MW00770223

Tempting God

Poems by Christopher Soden

LUCHADOR PRESS

Luchador Press

Big Tuna, TX

Copyright (c) Christopher Soden, 2023

First Edition 1 3 5 7 9 10 8 6 4 2

ISBN: 978-1-958182-49-9

LCCN: 2023947563

Cover image: taken from *The Sacrifice of Issac* by Michelangelo Caravaggio c/o the Uffizi Gallery

Title page image: *The Sacrifice of Isaac* by Julius Schnorr von Carolsfeld c/o the Columbia University Library

Author photos: Dan Rodriquez

Acknowledgments

The author would like to thank the editors of the following publications, where some of these poems previously appeared:

"heart of coal," "waffle house:" *Image Out*, "Pinocchio," "Not me," "Dance with Bones," "Redemption" "One very

dry, cold, perfect martini:" *Closer*, "The Last Picture Show:" *Vox Populi*, "Punchline," "somewhere in Brooklyn:" *The Good Men Project*, "Not Strangers:" *Chelsea Station*, "Original Sin:" *Ganymede*,

For Ann Howells, Lisa Huffaker, Daniel Verinder, Paul Koniecki, Ben Schroth, Jason Edwards, Dinah Waranch, Toni Alexander, Robin Turner, Joan Larkin, Lise Brown Alexander, Michael Simms, Lisha Garcia, Dave Wheeler, Jacinta Camacho Kaplan, Eduardo Corrall, David Townsend, Patrick Barth, Kathryn Levy, Jody Gladding, Frank Dunn, Cindy Huyser, Gene Verinder, Cindee Mayfield, Virginia Holloman, Leo Loyola, Richard Jackson, Leslie Ullman, Nance Van Winckel, Natasha Saje, Fran Carris, Logen Cure, Michael Puttonen, Brenda Gaba, Barbara Shinn, Gayle Bell, Patricia Golden, Frederick Mensch, David Agasi, Anita Barnard

Table of Contents

Prince of Broken Light

Cocksman

Beautiful Boys

For Jack Myers

For Joseph Natale and Peter Verrando

For Lon Rogers

For my cherished sisters: Victoria and Penelope

For Jason Ryberg who rose from the ashes to bring
this book to press

For Elizabeth Ross Soden: my brave, remarkable, sharp,
intelligent, mother. She had a daring sense of humor.
Mama you protected me fiercely, and I am prouder of
you than I can say. I love you mama.

And it came to pass, when he had made an end of speaking unto Saul, that the soul of Jonathan was knit with the soul of David, and Jonathan loved him as his own soul.

-1 Samuel 18:1

And as soon as the lad was gone, David arose out of a place toward the south, and fell on his face to the ground, and bowed himself three times: and they kissed one another, and wept one with another, until David exceeded.

-1 Samuel: 20: 1

Prince of Broken Light

Seachange

The other guys razzed me
for chasing skirt, but couldn't
deny I had the knack. I knew
what girls needed to hear
and how to pitch it. Last Tuesday
after lunch, some new guy
at school named Roger ducked

into the john for a Chesterfield.
His hair was coal black and curly.
His cologne sharp as cut lime
and cloves. I took the smoke
he offered and showed me how
to inhale without coughing. He could

have laughed, but he didn't.
That night Roger took me
to a Negro jazz club
called **Jelly Rolls,** where they
chuckled, and brought nasty
hooch, while the band jammed
to Count Basie and Cab Calloway.

He asked me about Thalia.
*Where do you touch? What
is her mouth like?* He grinned
and winked. *I'm starting to bone.*
There were sailors dancing slow
with their honeys, hair getting damp.
He said the lake was much cooler,

now it was so far into the night,
and we could talk
without shouting. Calm
and floating like terns

on a trade wind. The moon
was a luminous fossil,
and Roger joined me
when I left his blue Mustang
to aim a piss.

We used daffodils for a target,
dousing them and farting
like guys do. Breaking up
laughing. I climbed up next
to him on top of the trunk.
He started to sing Nat King Cole:
The dream has ended…..

then he tugged my zipper
and reached in. Tickling my cock
with two fingers. I socked his ear,
fiercely, but he just smiled.
His tongue wrapped in garlic
and onion and coffee bean.

I said, *Okay, Roger.* Sure, as I
thickened in his grip. Spunk
escaped in ragged jets. He
tucked his nose in the hollow
below my throat and ridiculous,
impossible tears got me

snotty and hoarse. He mopped
me with his hanky and I said
sorry for his ear. He began
to serenade me again
and I quit talking. His skin
turned to satin in blue moon
glow. I was gone for good.

Snake tango

Luke wasn't especially different
from the rest of us. We'd seen
blue eyeshadow, and black
mo-hawks before. Perhaps it was
Our Lady of Guadalupe on one
arm and *Lucifer* on the other.

Despite our supposed streetcred,
we were 13, and it was still
church camp, and Luke
might have been from Neptune.
He wasn't interested in a heart
stopping ice plunge

or predatory shudders
from archery or sudden tug
of angling. Maybe it was a
Wednesday I saw him hesitating
outside the Men's Showers. I
said, C'mon, Cowboy,

nothing to fear, but he insisted:
I'm not afraid, Nathan. We
shucked down, ditching
pungent clothes, jockey shorts
damp from last dribble drops

and boners. Other guys from
the cabin were crowding

under eight nozzles. Before long,
the strangeness of clustering
naked evaporated. Tossing

the shampoo, water spit-spouting,
aimless piss. Lunatic cocks
pinging and clapping, savoring
sud of lifebuoy buff. Luke dug
his journal (from the green trunk
under his bed) out for me,

scrawled with beguiling prayers
to copperheads. Vivid curses
in unknown languages,
to a dad with nothing
but a purple scowl and belt buckle.

The drawings of rabbits and goats
and frogs, chariots and reckless
wobbly rockets, canny jig between
tyrant Pentheus and deranged
God Dionysus. He found

a nook in my shoulder
before grieving broke him
open. Whether by accident
or intuition, I'd become

the storyteller for our cabin.
That night, as we settled
into our bunks, I told the guys
about my brother, Jakey.

How we knocked
this rolling rock off its axis,

every chance we got. Sneaking
off to Blues clubs till three,
breaking into houses, listening
for the delicate tick
of tumblers falling into place.

Sipping Maker's Mark, digging
on Brubeck and Monk, savoring
Havanas, content as pudgy Buddah,
till high and brights tipped us
off. Next day they started

with elbows to Luke's ribs
and ridiculous jokes cause you
just fucking need to laugh.
And naturally, male fart code,
and dirty songs, and frank,

spontaneous grins. I ducked into
the cabin, collapsing on my bed
and roared, drunk with relief,
tremors shaking my scrawny,
orphan body. I sang some
idiot tune. I sang for Lucas.

Permission

Easy to imagine the unspoken
terror that simmers
and rises from your gut
like magma turning and churning
the endless questions. The tingles
you conceal. They laugh at the boner
in the communal shower. The lingering
look that could trigger purple rage
or a black eye. The insistent pulse,
the rush of blood, like dizzy urgent
fever. The first time another guy returns
your intense gaze, you are jazzed
and panicked, the shadow that ached
to touch another peter suddenly
behind the wheel. Perhaps you follow
him home (parents still at work)
where you grab and toss and maybe
risk a tongue. Perhaps you just
look the other way. Whether or not you
continue the wordless, growling
consummations, the public beatings,
the loud ferocious ritual of defending
your maleness with the blood
of other men, goes on and on. Tango
of adrenaline, spit and soaking,
torn clothes. You join the marines,
still an undeniable badge, still a place
where so much salty, raw, swinging
cock makes it possible to confide:

You know buddy, if I were gay,
I'd be totally into you, without raising
a flag. When you return to Orlando,
you begin to scope out queer
night-clubs. Behavior of unashamed
faggots. Dykes. Watching them kiss and
caress. Then one night
you decide you must
bear witness. You must
save yourself.

You must block the exits.

Subversive

It was 1966. I was in 3rd grade.
I'd seen the New Wave
and liked the hair. So I let it
grow, unaware it would cause
such an uproar. My homeroom

teacher sent me to the office,
bobby pin in my hair.
The principal's secretary, read from
the Bible. Anarchy lost on me.

There was a beguiling older boy,
named Chris. Top of the totem.
I'd watch him sailing
between classes, as if some
dangerous God was nudging me.

He was 12, so tall his head
would brush gentle, congenial clouds.
Force jet planes to turn back.
I happened to pass him, ducking
in his locker, girlfriend

by his side. Slowly, a grin stretched
across his face like a crisp, white sail.
He walked up, and tousled me.
His girl smiling, too. *Look Chris,
it's just like yours.* A gush of bliss

shot through me, like rocket fuel.
Very cool, buddy, and instantly,
the cyclone I'd set in motion
was revealed, as an oracle,
and the shiny penny dropped.

Nicholas and Alexandra

Our whole family drove
to Houston, to spend Christmas
with my dad's mom. Father,
mother, and two older sisters.
Christmas Eve we finally agreed
on a movie. It was raining hard.
Cars splashing through
black, slick streets.

The spectacle of dying
Russian aristocracy, was a marvel.
The opulent, luminous gowns.
The somber, sophisticated tuxedos.
Enough servants to make a shtetl,
chaotic cosmos swirling
in counterpoint
to their masters, never colliding.

My sisters, Victoria and Penelope,
tortured one another. Vicki calm
and composed, Penny the frail yet
fearless Princess of *Sturm und Drang*.
We were a melange of intellect
and venom, despite our devotion
to the savior in the manger. Maybe

you know the rest, the child Alexei
bleeding from tender contusions,
and Rasputin, flagrant monastic

zealot, the only one
who could heal him.

When the Tsar and Tsarina,
Princesses and gentle Prince,
were ushered to the basement,
(spell holding till it was too late
to beg) none of us was surprised.
I think it was me who noticed

the sobbing that came
from Penelope, dragged to a film
with an ending she couldn't foresee.
Our clumsy attempts to comfort
her pointless, unable to explain
when she asked, *Why didn't you
say something?*

How could we tell her our
violent swim to the ocean of
starving ghouls ragged angry dog howls
was a foregone conclusion?

dwell in grace

the papa on television
doesnt get drunk
at home but still finds
ways to disappoint
the boy or his mother

she gets between them
and the ugly purple eye
of love i could never tell
when my dad
was sloshed or saw

when he met my sister
with a belt after a date
who was barely brave
enough to kiss her
long into the changing
hours i listen

to the naked ache of pop
(she brought home
on 45s) tonight i post
fragments of resignation
on social media: *"...dont let on,*

dont say shes broke
my heart..." and i will stop
now because none of this
matters it doesnt help

to wish we had smothered him
or sent him tumbling
down the 14 stairs
dividing our bedrooms
from the rest of the house

i talk to the television
i say *thank you papa*
or im sorry dad or thats
ok son and choke

Prince of broken light

I would have liked a dad
who grinned, who carried me
boisterously, instead of the growling
psychopath, unbuckling
his belt, face purple like beets.

If I hadn't closed him off, my brain
would have cooked
like an egg. I wasn't rugged.
He should have put me in a dress.
He should have knocked me
into next week. I should have found
him sleeping and slit his throat.

My sister Vicki was dating when I
was still a boy. She brought home
a guy named Jake. When she
introduced us, without a signal
I could recognize, he hoisted me

to his shoulders. I was shrieking,
limbs akimbo. Jake my lanky tower
of congeniality. Rangy brother
of the moment. I'm so sorry, man.

My buddies in cub scouts were:
Paul, Brad, Russell, David. Invited
to swim in a private pool, I saw
how easy they slid from their clothes,

piling them, cocks like crooked
metronomes. They could tell
I was hanging back but smiled
graciously. *It's OK Chris.* But
I couldn't undress. Outside

there was a soda fountain.
Unconsciously I mimicked
the way mother spoke
to other women. The den
mothers giggled. I tried mixing
syrups, but it made me puke.

When I was six I changed
in the Men's Dressing Room
at Kidd Springs, where I saw
three teenage boys, gangly
and jazzy and carelessly light.

How intuitively they peeled
sopping trunks, wringing them,
cheerful clappers swanging
and rocking with brush of black hair.
Flagrantly drying deep asses, planets

from a zillion faraway suns clobbering
my skull. Boy engine flowering
and clenching and violently drumming.
Drowning in rough, subversive glory.

o i am wobbly lightning rod
prince of broken light uninitiated

hopfrog supple and aching
for untouchable brothers i am gods

grimy ridiculous cowboy
imposter in shower cluster
aimlessly pissing needing
a buddy to scrub my back
i am the son shaming his dad
naked   tiger   naked   monkey   naked   waif

Punchline

I cannot tell you why I picked
Barbra Streisand, the first time
I bought an album. Or why
I chose the lavender shirt,
or watch with leather cuff,
or I guess, what might have been

considered long hair for a 15-year-old
boy visiting Mexico for the first time.
I obsessed over these questions,
and though my trip was filled
with queasy, melancholy revelations,
one in particular went undetected.

Not the grisly crucifixes with unforgiving
saviors, martyrs crawling to *Our Lady
of Guadalupe*, the defiant Rivera murals,
vivid with corruption and anarchy.

Not the rainy evenings reading (while
grownups bounced from club
to club for rum and jazz)
about Lenny Bruce, notorious,
bisexual comic mainlining smack,

covering windows with foil to block
vestigial sunlight. I wondered what I
might have done, or said, when
the customs official told me to step

into a small room, where he gingerly
squeezed my crotch, watching
my response. I was puzzled
but not alarmed, figuring
it was just another guy
thing, outside my realm

of the uninitiated. This was
before I understood what
he thought he knew, or why
things happen in the world,
or that the reason for anything
doesn't matter.

Like a stone

I leave the Christmas matinee
after five. Clouds sparse and dark
blue, fierce wind kicking up
from the North. Last night
I rented *Midnight Cowboy*, hoping
it wasn't a mistake. The first time

I saw, I was spending the night
with Frederick, my closest friend,
who lived in the dorm. Some guys
trapped me in the men's toilets,
blocking the door, forcing the air
from my lungs. But how

could I not? With goofy Joe Buck,
cowboy hustler who cares
too much to earn genuine coin
for sex; and Ratso hobbling
(like Amahl or Tiny Tim)
and that inconsolable harmonica

and Nilsson dragging me
to endless aching? How badly
I need Christmas this time
around. Something to keep me
from slugging myself. Ratso
follows me like a cozy shadow,

all crumby and disgusting. If only I
could kiss him on the mouth again
and again, crash the showers
in the men's dorm and lather him
tenderly. If only I could go back. If
only Frederick had said something.
Just something.

snakes and ladders

in the cold dark
brick and stone

uncoiling smoke
of elementary

indoctrination
with textbooks

and snotrags ready
to beat the singing

right out of you
i found a boy

skin pale and milky
as the sun burning

through gray clouds
simon spoke

with a lilt gliding
spirit of air

that crossed the glistening
ocean from the realm

of fairies dark
winged and defiant

and busy with fizzy
mischief we couldn't have

exchanged more than
three or four sentences

my heart incapable
of surviving

the undiluted deluge
the day i found him

at recess with a gift
for a chipper

brother hardly more
than a stranger

i knew it was nothing
just a board game

from the five and dime
fifty years later i still cannot

imagine what he thought
when i said this is for you

but it doesn't matter
because his smile

was the nameless
extravagance

of boy love

Cocksman

Dance with Bones

He offers to buy my next drink,
but I've seen him many times
in the past and cordially
decline; not bothering
to object when he pulls out
the empty chair lingering
next to me. He doesn't notice
when vodka stingers pour
from his ribcage or smoke
from his Winston seeps out
his jaw. He's selected "Happy
Together" eight times now
and I say, "Okay, but please,
pick something else."
He's a sloppy drunk,
and grazes my ass with tinny
fingers, breathing disgusting
suggestions down my ear.
I let him kiss me
out of pity, understanding
he'd use his tongue if he could.
He tells me he's mastered
the delicate art of using teeth
in fellatio, and promises depravity
of the most ecstatic sort. The last
time I went home with him
it was unforgettably vile. He was
behind and I was facing the wall,
panting like a beagle. I don't know

what he was using but believe
it must have been a dildo
made of ice. Shudders
and violent seizures. He chuckled
and bit my shoulder.
I'm guessing everyone has told you
the Reaper is a great cocksman
and okay, he was, he was.
But after a while, copulating
on gravestones, breaking
into mortuaries, loses its punch.
After a while he's just another
mope with a boner who never
wants to go home.

Two wolves

for Davey

I introduce myself to the young
Korean woman ringing cash
in the gift shop for the New
York Museum of Modern Art,
but it is no use. Less than
five minutes listening
to my buddy Davey and she
barely realizes I'm there.

She is his. He knows exactly
what to notice: *There's no one
here to help you? How long
have you been in town?* Questions
only the concerned and intrigued
would ask. Eight people waiting
and she proffers her number

without a second thought. He lives
with a voluptuous, sharp Latina
and turns to me later, asking
forbearance for his indiscretion.
But it wasn't necessary. Two hours
ago we engaged on the fourth floor
with collages and engravings.

A multimedia piece broadcasting
locations from the artist's body
on a cluster of small, closed-circuit

screens. Blue waves skipped
and blipped across live captures
of his wrist, nipple, throat, eye,

his penis. Davey would confide
when a woman sent his blood down
the chilly, dark current and wanted
to know when a guy did the same
for me. *Tall drink in green*

High Tops. By the Man Ray. Slender
naiad in blue silk. For us
it wasn't predatory, but sacrament
of miraculous hues and vibrant
tastes finally revealed. If only

one time I'd told him just how
exquisitely the realms of wish
and ponder, fragrance and yearning
rocked open for me in his company.

Just chatting, watching him
shave or feeling his lips grace
my cheek. But I imagine
he knows. You could ask me
something, wise, like, *How does*
love mean? What does it do?

And I could say when
the shadow world comes to gobble
and smack. When the hours
groping upward stretch beyond

and beyond into moments and ticks
too numerous to fathom. I know
there is a voice, eager to sail the
empty miles of space, waiting
to blend with familiar notes
of mine. Together we sing
to the moon, immediate
and unattainable.

heart of coal

days fall and fall
black rain in spring

equinox daring me
to forget caution

to baptize myself
in defiance leaping

rowdy in downpour
fearless enough to taste

tender shell above
pink lobe below

another guys kiss
bearing weary moxie

heat lightning
of sour ash and bourbon

the shudder of nuzzling
deep pungent notch

gut chuckles mixed
with bristling rough

whisker against belly
against blade

i slowly drop
my lids and call

upon the father
before all fathers

tapping intuitive grace
ignoring arrogance

of thumpers and rollers
and cross burners

reaching for the torn
blessing of forbidden

intimacy the bliss
of the infinite

dip the comfort
of familiar musk

monkey brothers

tom and i arcing
our rowdy boy
college days swimming
inktide of nightfall
leaping and diving
and bellowing jaunty songs
of spunk and catastrophe

the famished kiss
the finality of *no*

love came easy to tom

and i the comfort
of his arms tucking me
in a rugged hug but
somehow a flaw a bruise
of the skull a ragged spell

washed over us like blue
milk from the moon that night
was broken glory bourbon flirting
with vestiges of muddled
paradise and we stumbled
into toms new flat giddy

saunter of the inebriated
our beds a welcome blur
hours later i navigated the cool

dark to release a piss i found
my fractured buddy kneeling

at the toilet resigned
to violent cure of puking
rusty red hair sprouting
from the nook of his ass

you sleep naked i asked
and he said *yeah* rising
to rinse his mouth
i understood drifting
off easier with jangler
spilling unabashed

and id never seen him
before without clothes fierce
and friendly cock bouncing
sprawl of bushy pit tender belly
and jolted by his sanguine flush
his exquisite gangly frailty
i came apart

Tantalizing

If I tell you sometimes bisexual
guys are worse. I'm not sure
it explains anything,
but I will say it. Just the same.
Before I met Tim
I believed my attraction

to other men was a symptom
or cycle. Perhaps a way to secure
the intense love I craved
from other guys, or a safe step
that would ultimately end
in consummating with women.

It was only after a long summer
evening of sipping Stoli and lime,
listening to 50's radio, relaxing
with a slow progression
of smokes. That he suggested we

jack off together. My blood
steeped like Vesuvius. I finally
understood something crucial
about myself. Ironically I didn't
grasp Tim's penchant for fomenting
damage, or watching you suffer;

like a thrush caught blindly
banging in an endless black flue.

But he had other gifts.
One evening in the windy, desolate,
shrubby college town of Lubbock,

Texas, we were dining
in a small restaurant
specializing in steaks. He had
an idea and we visited the
Men's Room. Not unusual
considering the establishment,

it had one toilet, one urinal,
no partition and a lock
on the door. Smaller
than some closets. He wanted
to swap underwear. Nothing else.
Just a glimpse of his pale ass,
the moist warmth of boxers,

the faint odor of piss. Tim gave me
shared experience of peters. Twins.
Doppelgangers one to another.
It was dangerous and careless
and creepy and brotherly
and he blew off
the back of my skull.

Noah and his sons

The vineyard dad planted took hold
swiftly, and crept like mad, a marvel
of sacrifice and quickening sap.
One summer evening when the air
was drowsy with gaping, seductive

flowers, papa decided to gulp some
of that silky wine. Who knows
what men will do after sweet poison
slides down the gullet, spreading
down their limbs like a giddy snake?

I heard my father roaring
a song and capering
ridiculously as he fell
into the tent. After twenty minutes
I yanked past the heavy flap

to say *hush now*, and found
him naked, sprawled on his bed.
Chest thatched like a great lumbering
bear, root draped carelessly
down his thigh, swarthy

as a plum. I said
a kind of prayer. Whistling
at its heft, weighing it
in my palm, I left father
to the phantasmagorical
fathoms of slumber.

Shem and Japheth could see
I was off balance and lost.
When we bathe, we giggle and tug,
scritching each other's scalps,
groaning happily, buffing shoulders
and spines. But how was this different?

Dad's stone cold drunk. He's naked.
I held it. You held what?
Shem slugged me and I
bent over, heaving, scalding
salt blearing my eyes.

Japheth grabbed a blanket off
a donkey and they walked backwards
into the tent, concealing our father's
shame, without a glimpse.
Next day they told him
what happened. I saw him ignite

the incense burner. His outcry
summoning *Alochim.* Pronouncing
the curse on me and all
my progeny thereafter. I pled
with him to reconsider. I was nudged

by awe and curiosity. My need
to be closer. *It didn't mean anything,*
Papa. Had my brothers not
intervened, his unbridled thrashing
would have sent me
to the land of the dead.

Original Sin

I couldn't say no when Trevor turned
the storage shed into an altar
where he shifted objects and ignited
the Coleman lantern, never letting
the flame up too high.
There were French playing cards

and Viceroys at the start. After awhile
we played poker for clothes, when I still
understood nothing of the world,
unable to imagine what two naked boys
could do but chuckle and fart.

He would think of stupid games
like "Report Card" or "Uncle's Lesson"
or "Kept After School." Tell me to watch
Jesus, heart wrapped in garlands
of thorn and flame or Our Blessed Virgin
Mother (images taped to the wall,

looking back) while I bent across his lap
or clutched my ankles. It was astonishing,
how he summoned the elements: melodically,
spontaneously, casting a spell. I tried
to disengage (even as blows returned

me to my bone cage) noticing details
that never caught my attention before.
The rich magnificent layers of refuse

that transformed our clubhouse
into a kingdom of spider nest
and ghost eggs. Clusters of slick shining

hatchlings that could fill your body
in a day. Spit-paper dwellings
for wasp and hornet, shriveled purple
cadaver of what might have been
a rabbit or raccoon or possum before it lost

to teeth or time. It's too easy to say
it was not so bad. The tingle I felt
or wisdom I bring with me now
to the bed, the bar, the alley, the warm
wet dock houses with jewel-eyed
invisible witnesses. Hushed

comfort of surf. You never felt
the cold dread in your gut
when Trev showed up
ringing your doorbell, over and over,
determined to deliver
the beating you always knew
was coming.

waffle house

stuck here somewhere
between san bernadino
and amarillo where
the jukebox keeps playing
nat king cole over
and over and nobody
seems to notice the waitress
bears a passing resemblance
to gloria grahame asks
if i want *gravy*
with those hash browns
darlin keeps refilling
my creamy green coffee
mug giving me the smile
waitresses reserve
just for orphans
the calendar with the blue tractor
has not been replaced
since the year my father
died some stray mutt
outside by the milk bottles
is commiserating
with the man
in the moon the drunk
at the counter has maybe eaten
three bites of stew
and sings along with the juke
a very strange enchanted boy
stumbles over to me

with four days growth
and worn black gabardine
and sour smell like something
you left in the fridge last easter
and the cook doesn't care
and gloria doesn't care
and the mutt and the moon
do not care and its 4am
and yes
i kiss him yes

Nobody wants to be friends with Jakey

He might phone around two
in the morning or drink with you
till you both get kicked out
for brawling or puking or singing
too loud. Jakey is sloppy
and his manners aren't for shit.
He'll piss right next to you
in the alley, farting
without apology or flip off
a cop who wants to pull you over.
If someone insults you, he won't
stop pummeling till they taste blood.
If they threaten, Jakey will be grabbing
a shovel from the trunk of his
vintage black Mustang convertible.
If you're hungry he'll lift the chops
from somebody else's plate or show you
how to walk the check like a pro.
He's not ashamed when you catch him
snoring during *The Magic Flute* or a revival
of Warhol's early underground films.
Downing absinthe or chasing the dragon's
tail at *Camille's*, he grabs you
when a tango commences, dropping
to a dangerous and delectable dip.
When he seals his agonized confession
with a blazing, toxic, reptilian kiss,
laughter explodes from your lungs
like nuclear fission. You bite

his shoulder hard, your left
hand gripping his ribcage, the right
one reaching for his fly.

The Curveball of Silent Beauty

I could describe the color
of his hair, his eyes (if I could
remember) his pale skin, his
diminutive height. But no. For me
his anger was remarkable. The tacit

seething, tangible and canny
as bubbling pitch, a double-shot
of Jaegermeister, a blackout
in an August heatwave. He'd
befriended his rage, it never left

his side. The charisma of his shadow
was intoxicating. Everyone said he
was bad news. His friends did. I told
God I didn't care. I believed we

shared a primitive connection.
I jerked off over him. Three times.
It was quick, vivid, intuitive,
gorgeous. A blind fever
cracking my skull. There was

no life after that. Just fierce jangle-
jungle: gobbling sleep, clarity,
simple quiet pleasure
of Amaretto, a sophisticated film,
a rich bite of gravlax. Our last residency,

he was actually magnanimous.
He hugged me. More than once.
Front row for my lecture, my reading.
Met my mother at graduation. Took
a picture together. Just he and I.
Scalding tears on the flight back.

We could talk about the violent
ride of misunderstanding. Delusion.
The beating lurking behind
the unspoken. I never heard anything

back. Not a single word. I am
the Prince of Ridiculous. The Sworn
Enemy of Reason. The Pathetic
Monkey of Cannibal Dads. It's OK
to laugh now. I would.

Tempting God

for Andrew

Gobsmacked to see him
jogging that towering, dangerous
highway loop, tempting fate. Sopping
from fierce triple digit summer,
his brother supposed to pick him up.
He apologized for the sweat
on my upholstery but I reassured
him. Some encouraging scripture
from Joshua stretched inside
his right arm. His name was Andrew.
Training for a boxing match, he was
shirtless, tooth gone, ribs bending
to make a boat from caramel skin.
I was drowning in sweet reek
of ass and pit. *You're a handsome one,*
I said, his polite chuckle boycode
for gentle rejection. He could not
have been more humbled
or grateful. Startling
among males. We know only
to pound pound pound
your way to proof. To earn
our rocking, implacable balls.
I could not believe how close
I got (bloody nose or not)
to offering him the rough
miracle of a man's mouth.
But then, I couldn't. Andrew

trusted sweetness more
than most men. Why would I not
rescue him from the fatality
of milky heat? How could I not
open my door to this intersection
of liquid sunstroke
and ferocious dance?

How could I not?

How could I not?

Pad Thai

I wasn't happy to leave the comforting
arms of photographers and sculptors.
Painters and potters. Playwrights
and poets I found at the artist's colony

in Vermont. But my excursion
was done and a plane waiting
to gulp me the next day,
and return to Texas. So I
checked into a motel in Burlington.

No elevator. No room service.
I ordered something from Jade Reed,
a place I'd never heard of.
I made the trek for ice and pop,
climbing the weary stairs

to the room that was just mine,
and undressed, changing. I discovered
a tv documentary flamboyant
with details of Harrison, Lennon, McCartney
and Starr. It was November and I
parted the orange curtains, somber

with the vexation between Texas,
and anything enchanted and careless
as snow. Was it a young, sweet lad
who rapped shyly at my door?
His smile was without pretense
or effort, my spontaneous flirtation

graciously accepted. Jazzed
by my chipper messenger
(fetching as Hermes) I opened
my styrofoam package of puzzle
and wonders. Delivered the strange

concoction to my mouth.
Closing my eyes to get
the full effect. Ecstatic waves
suffused my blood, forehead to heel,
palm to shoulder, mansac to ass.

Sitar music unwound, like radio
transmission from another galaxy.
Drizzling sticky bliss
in my ear: *I once met*
a boy, or should I say,
he once met me? And then,

without notice, impossible
tatters, weightless as prayer, drifted
to my sill. In that moment
of intersection, the earth
was a glad and remarkable
home, swaddling me
in the promise of miracles
within reach.

Goodnight, honey

She wasn't crazy about the insipid
platinum blondes she was asked
to play, sop to buffoons,
a goddess too merciful
to see she could turn
them to ashes, or orangutans
with a murmured spell.

Her last film was *The Misfits:*
written by her husband: a woman
in pigtails and jeans, frank
and naive. Blind to the effect
she has on cowboys as lost
as she. She finds them trapping
defiant mustangs, and fights
them off, before they can break

another soul. In *The Seven Year Itch*
she straddles a subway grate, steam
lifting her skirt like the hot breath
of a Minotaur or drooling neighbor.
In *Some Like it Hot* she plays ukulele
in a women's band, crossing paths
with two musicians, disguised
as ladies. She's done with guys

who squander her money
on the ponies, and other girls.
Sleeping that first night

on the train, the bass player climbs
into the upper bunk. Drunk
on enchantment, he wishes her

goodnight. *Goodnight, Honey*,
she replies, in that whispery
way, softer than moonlight.
For that moment, this
orphan of the world splurges
without caution, warmth impossible

to find. In that astonishing
instant, gone before we know,
actual care brushes
our cheek, but lingers
as long as we let it.

Not strangers

When a woman answered
the door, I understood Rick
was different. It was after 2
in the morning. "I don't judge you
boys," she said earnestly
in her East Texas drawl and went
to wake him. I asked if I could

use his shower, kept the door ajar
as his bathroom light was broken.
He was polite and sweet, asking for
one of my smokes, if I was married.
In 30 years of seeing escorts
and masseurs none of them

asked me that. "Oh. No." I replied.
He was not a certified massage therapist,
but he'd read some books.
He said it helped as they'd cut
his wife's hours waiting tables.

I asked if he would remove
his shorts. He chuckled when I
felt his dick. Like he didn't expect
it, but didn't care. He didn't yell
or hit me. It wasn't a bad rub,
and he didn't mind that I was fat

and lying on the bed where he
and his wife slept, and yes, probably
made love. When he began to finish
me I reached around to squeeze
his firm, downy, ass,
improving the arc. We stretched

out, smoking, talking easily.
A local television show was looking
for extras in town and his friends
said he looked like Edward Norton,
and you know, it was true.

I haven't had enough money
to see him again but remember
driving home in that sudden
calm of post-climax and tobacco,

spontaneous embrace afterward,
thinking something about impossible
grace. The streets never seemed
so empty and quiet.

Beautiful Boys

Redemption

A lad you can't identify
on your voicemail confesses.
I had a dream of flight.
Mama has kissed you
goodnight and you wake to
discover a naked boy
weeping, in the nursery.

He comes from a place unknown
to you. Second star to the right,
and straight on till morning.
You will help him reconcile
to his shadow, and he will
guide you in the discipline
of intuition and loft.

You are sooty and daft
and remarkable. You belong
to no one. Listen. Big Ben
is counting down to the end
of your sorrow. Only just this
moment comes the changing hour.
One-two-three…

The nursery window gapes.
The skyline of London awaits.
Your jig shakes loose
like a wet schnauzer.
You were not made to fall.
You can fly. You can fly. You can fly.

okay okay

there are fragments
of me aching

to resolve this black swim
this imbecilic metronome

dragging my spirit between
healing and harm

kiss and spit pillow
and rock how might i

have imagined this
meticulous crawl

through gelatin fathomless
elaborate trance that cradles

and confounds while i try
to climb in bed with my anger

or share my delicate infinite
moonbeam soup tucking

it between his weary lips
spoon by spoon gulp

by gulp my chuckles
gorgeous and slower

than forgiveness rapacious
as regret why do we

strip completely down
for friction for comfort

to embrace strangeness
of the flesh

the awful miraculous
delight of blurring

where you begin and the
other ends i place

my nightmares
on your trembling altar

i stretch and swallow i shut
my lids and say *okay okay*

Not me

Maybe I'm on I-30, headed for home,
or waiting my turn at Tom Thumb
with rice and Cokes and Fig Newtons.
Maybe I'm next at the dentist
and something comes on the radio. Something

stupid. Okay? It's not Handel's *Messiah*
or some choir with a lofty message
about salvation and redemption. And I'm
not some fucking rube. I live in town,
with the traffic and phony light and cement.

And I've heard them all dozens of times,
since before I could walk, just like everybody
else. So maybe I'm leafing through *Time*
or *USA Today* wondering how
I'm gonna pay my water bill this month,

and I hear some lame crap about shepherds
or mystics chasing down an oracle, or this kid
sleeping in a feeding trough. Like I'm sure
a baby's gonna care. Yeah. I know.
The "irony" of a savior starting out

in a barn. Whatever. But somehow
the words are seeping into one ear,
because I'm distracted, as I said,
and a line drops through
to the bottom of the black ocean. You see?
I can't explain it. I have no gift

to bring. In that moment, I see
this blizzard of pitch and muck
and shit we crawl through
every day, everybody just shoving
and biting and beating on each other.

Nobody able to find enough time
or room to just be decent
to someone. Anyone. All you hear
is how they can't fucking stand you,
because your car died
in rush hour traffic, or your kid

is crying, or you need
a box of macaroni that isn't broken.
You're just something else
wrong in their lives. Another kind
of torment. Then I think of God,

squeezing through this curtain.
This crushing, massive curtain
of hurt and detachment and rage.
This world, this world, this world

that smacks you and chews you
to pieces all the fucking time
and God pushing through
like some greased up maniac
crossing the English channel

or silver catfish gliding down
the stewy swamp, just to make sure

we know we're not forgotten
and I'm thinking.
Why? What difference
does it make? I'm nothing special.

I'm just another guy. Another prick.
It's too late. You can't do this.
Not for me. Not me. And yeah.
Then I just break, just break,
just break. Completely down.

Destitute

for mama

There's something that feels destitute
about watching crows scrounge
for scraps of bread
on a rough day in January
when the wind is fierce
and brusque and grass

famished while I wait
inside the car at Sonic. Things are
not so bad. I can still afford
a cheeseburger or ice cream
scoop, when I ache for a treat

and don't begrudge those
fabulously black iridescent
scavengers their crust of respite
from someone done with lunch,
or stuff turned beyond human
consumption. I have no quaint

appreciation for dainty sparrows
dipping at crumbs or canary divas
pecking at seed biscuit. This afternoon
when the sky is smudged
and listless, I feel like a shit
not tipping the sweet kid

who skates up. Though I chose
this place to save
some coin, when my spirit needs
to believe in beneficence. I look
into his eyes that forgive me,

and say *hang on* as I unbuckle
my belt, sifting through
a thousand squashed cups
and faded yellow wrappers
for some shining dime or quarter.

Nebbish

He was hitchhiking when I stopped
on the expressway, head wrapped
in bandages, wisdom teeth extracted.
He'd run out of money
for bus fare, his mother too busy
to take him to the dentist. Despite
salt throb and disorientation, he offered
to pay for my gas, once his paycheck came.

We worked together at **Taylor's** Books,
and just like me, he took his turn
at the cash registers, shelving, helping
customers on the phone and floor.
30 minutes for lunch. He had a mop
of hair the color of molasses, brush

mustache and googly, Mad Scientist
glasses. He might have been
a bit slow to catch on,
and sometimes, fray your nerves.
But vigilant as a Franciscan monk,
and not a drop of harm in him.

Veronica was our manager. Proud
and slender as a cornstalk. Amber
honeycomb hair. Moonbeam
skin clustered with freckles.
Cunning as a hawk. Do I need
to explain he irritated Veronica,

or that she fired him, with no
prospects ahead? She could have

cracked the planet like an egg
and gobbled it raw, but instead chose
to devour a chipper, innocuous soul,
because she wanted to. Because she could.
I thank our Father, watching

across the black, bone-chilling
cosmos, for putting me there.
Blood jamming gauze-packed jaw,
as he sat next to me in the car,
oblivious to the cruelty
done to him. But perhaps
that's for the best.

cutie pie

chloe and i get a late start
on errands sun gone
translucent moon
drifting over faintest sky
traffic starting to crunch
chloe puts her paws
on the wheel and in due
diligence i thank her
for easing my obligations
i stroke her soft coat
deliver three kisses
to her nose asking myself
if she wonders or simply
says *this is a yes*
from papa i do not want
to drown you in the black
heavy molasses of cutie pie
it is only i need her
to understand she matters
and if not possible then
something however rough
and ridiculous and inept
from this catastrophe
we scramble and scratch
she and i two creatures
fortunate enough to welcome
the others company
so if foolish ritual gives me
opportunity to let her know

shes the best fucking driver
on the road i will wolf down
that scrap from gods bag
of magic tricks and turn
it to the supper of all
gracious things as we chew

Kitchen Duty

In this docile and earnest
community of craftsmen, I have been
fortunate enough to elicit: a bed,
a lamp, a chair in the dining hall
where most of us take our turn
in work exchange for scholarship.

I was relieved, cleaning steel tubs
and skillets and saucepans and utensils
for the respite and consumption
of our many. Nothing to break.
Fine shiny Medusa-curl scrubber

for scorched clangy cumbersome
stockpot and waxy crust of potato.
I dunk colander into proliferating
dash of lacquered protozoan bubble chain.
Slick eddies of congealed iridescence,

clouds evincing from gush and rush
of hot hot hot too hot, more cold more cold
glurshing flush of splatter from tap,
fiercely rub and sclosh soothing gold
molten downpour rinse, trajectory
of propulsion's flower, springling

to cut film of soap, vestigial cringe
of pink liquid neon while jammin
and pouring my grief into world stew

with Ricky Bragg, Lou Reed, Van Morrison,
Leonard Cohen and Anita Baker. Soaking

trousers down from my waist, tee-shirt
halfway to my navel. Foam and crud
wash up past elbow to reach
for sweet glob of Thai Peanut Sauce
under iron casserole where Mark
(gustatory god of clashing and calamitous
cosmos) cultivates luxurious sacrament
of demonstrable bliss. Temples stream,

spectacles fog and shift, as scalp dampens
from this laboratory of trouble and poach.
Where light is unmuted and flowage
a break, a break, a break. Shallow tubs
for salad components stack and nest

in smaller sink to my left, on chopping
block and counters. Cookie sheets
half my size drop into ooky gumbo
of scrap bitten cheese crumb, butter, cider,
Brussels sprouts and carrot sleet quagmire,
needing another installment of delicious,

scaldy, voluminous froth billow, raucous
glory of lather bath for tong and spatula,
measuring cup and buffet trough. Rough
rapture in polish dry of countless
terry dishtowels, scruffy cloth to buff

and rummage for the least visible
glint of moisture. I am Prince Rhapsodoodle.
Sultan of Sud. I coddle each vessel
with meticulous sop. Panoramic blizzard
of feather storm. I wield my radiance
extravagantly, coaxing brave metallic

gloss from bowl, cake pan, ladle.
Supple white and blue cloth creased
and fastidious as a Bride of Christ
Splendiferous howl of the mindless!
Ecstatic dance of the daffy!

Lush comfort of knowing they stack
and wait for me tomorrow after
tomorrow until I reconcile finally
with the irreducible inescapable
moment before me. Basking in
the glorious *now!*

house of yes

everything is white
the air cool avant-
garde piano music
(soothing french)
asserts itself
passively its source
impossible
to determine
there is plenty
of ice and clear pure
bottles of effective vodka
rum gin fresh lemon
and cocktail glasses
that might be
assimilated sculpture
you notice after the host
has handed you
a scintillating
beverage taken you
in his arms delivering
a brimming kiss (glorious
hair the shade of cayenne
red you've always
imagined) he recognizes
your ache and after all this
is the house of yes
where love gushes
like the milky cure
to all poisons

and nothing is wrong
every motive every wish
daffy with spilling
jubilation and fallibility
the closest anyone
comes to harm
it doesn't matter
in the house of yes
clarity swallows
every tear an infinite
liquid nimbus

Cocktail

An abscess sprouted
at the back of my thigh
where I couldn't see,
so the doctor put me on
strong antibiotics. So loopy,
I lost track
of my psychotropics. Leaving

Jack in the Box with Chloe
on my lap, I felt a flood
wash through my brain.
As if the earth
no longer tolerated
my presence. I had to snap

off the radio and pull over,
scalding salt brimming. Black
cyclone gulping me
straight to its maw. There's nothing

cozier than the cocktail
Janice and I have found
together through the months.
The seasons. One combination
after another, juggling
and swimming and balancing

till precision emerged. I have
learned to appreciate the ritual

of the small red box, with seven
hatches. Counting one or two
per day, blue or yellow

or orange, tiny writing, scored,
numbered, saving capsules
for the last. It's not about
a cure, its finally knowing
you can manage. It's embracing
the revelation that a small
prescription bottle rolling

under the sofa could send you
spinning. I no longer fear
addiction. I have discovered
grace of quantifiable comfort.
I take my miracles where I can
find them.

somewhere in brooklyn

another me is
listening
to billie holliday
nursing a pipe
sipping
makers mark
steeping
in a tub
of deliciously hot
water steam clouds
thicker than heaven
muscles unwinding
a guy with pitch
black hair and coke
bottle glasses kisses
me ferociously
as if nothing else
mattered somewhere
in brooklyn regret
is a country
i have never seen
dense soup with garlic
balsamic vinegar
and pungent ginger
graces the air
my heart brims
and tears sparkle
from the alley
a ragged tomcat
serenades us

set me gently

on my raft and float
me down the cool
cool river i am
ready to surrender
to sublime absence
of focus release
of care
let giddy moon
climb far beyond
my reach
let air grow thick
let toads welcome
me on my supple
whisper journey
through the gates
of lost gravity and regret
let bandages of fat melt
evaporate
till i am essence
of essence of joyful
boyself light
and nimble jazzy
and impervious to dread
let my bones dance
like chopsticks
in a bowl of noodles
let my heart bounce
like foolish yellow
kite in empty
foreverness
of sky

Pinocchio

Pinocchio has left Geppetto
for the splendid, teeming world
of thunder and phenomena, smoke
and red buttons, lather of hops.
Blind to the miracles swimming

inside his hobbly body, child of wings
and bells, bred of a blue air nymph
and a woodcarver's despair. He has
found a job in the theatre, feature performer

amongst the marionettes. Dancing
with other puppets. The only one
that is not a sham, exactly. He is
surrounded by jointed dolls
who began as he did, as wood,

but cannot truly reason or act,
learn or regret, only echo
the vibration of soul tremors.
Druggy confection of red candy

hearts. We are privy to
some sacred gag, watching
this dope, this enchanted
hunk of timber strutting and capering:
I got no strings to hold me down,
and know this is sad, though we are

not sure why. Time enough to find
the lonely place, with no constraint
or tether, of those who will miss
our company if we must work late,
or bail us out of jail, or let us

know if we're being selfish,
or unkind, or not getting enough sleep.
Time enough for this green stone
adrift in the cornerless realms
of black galaxies, to cut us loose
to the land of angels, goblins, sprites.

Where cold beauty and sparkly
charm waft upward, like the songs
of departed immortals, groping
for God's tender care. What favor
overtook Pinocchio when that blue goddess
stirred his molecules, when stolid oak
became sentient to taste
the exquisite misery
of insouciance, of wings and bells?

There are no strings on me.

Frailty

God, this is no good,
teetering, wobbling
groaning like some
fucking fossil, brittle
and pathetic. *Why bring
me here?* This once bright
and dappled world,
recoiling, slipping
like shadow.
No more sweetness.
Only memory of lush
crush of blackberry, palpable
cloud of beaten cream.
Films that bring
the unfathomable
cup of despair quench
me like a feckless sot.
So I wail, so I bellow
and thrash against the current.
So the pottery isn't safe
around me. So strangers
puzzle at me, an alphabet
that might have come
from Pluto or Saturn.
Father dip me
please in churning chill
of frosty joysplosh.
Jostle my joints
like maracas, hug me

with thunderclap crown me
with peonies. Send
a thousand sailors
to my door. To kiss me
with sizzle of heat
lightning. Help me
shake off
discouragement
like a wet spaniel.
Leave grief for another
day. No more eclipse,
no more ash, no more
surrender.

Please.

Swaddling

When you put on your coat
and light a smoke
on the front stoop, December
gusts tear into you. But
that drag rides all the way
down as you shut your lids.
A hat like your dad
wore when he thrummed
his bass at the clubs, skitters
down the street, no one
to chase and bring it back.
For the first time you notice
a distant train bellowing
like a bull past consolation.
A man in his 20's wanders
under a streetlamp, snuffling
now unmistakable. You offer
your handkerchief
but the wind is fierce
and deafening. The night enfolds
him like an endless black
curtain. You barely make out
the whimper you follow
for blocks, until you find
a spaniel too afflicted
to stand. Why is tonight
different? Saturday or Wednesday
you'd have returned home.
But now, at 10:37, something

rough bruises your chest.
You remove your jacket
and wrap him
delicately, singing
in a whisper. You bend
to kiss his sloppy snout.
Now something turns
your bones to light.

One very cold, dry perfect martini

for Peter Verrando

I remember the drink
from our father's age. By the time
I reached six, I knew how the husband
ended his daily labors, and invoked
his rest. The door to dreamland
in a frosty, conical glass: World
of our fathers, Pete. Though I
knew this was not a nightly ritual

in my own home, I watched enough
television to know, this is what
they would choose if they could.
Dick Van Dyke, Danny Thomas, Carl Betz,
Honey, I'm Home, and don't forget
Hugh Hefner and **Playboy after Dark**. This was

the conjugal bell, the daddy call,
we all recognize. Mama brushed her hair,
pinched on earrings, *Darling*.
He tastes her, briefly, with eclat.
She hands him the canny, delicate vessel
with it's one green eye, cool and neat
and potent and unspoken and urbane.

This is your express ticket, your life
begins again with this drink.
And there is jazz and caresses and subdued
smiles. The last time your folks visited

from New York, you showed your dad
the bottle of Gordon's and the grin opened

his face like a quiet firecracker. If my heart
were to clamber towards some counterfeit
of gratitude, Peter, it would be those times
we shared the small, dissolute
hours after evening had cast off and before
the sun crept. We are punchy and fevered

and conversation carries us far
from the dock of our ordinary lives.
We never tire of the other's sweet,
dreamy soliloquy, the hand extended
to coax and fish the salty portal,
to let the squalling pipsqueak gorge
his tiny roiling bellows. Here is mecca.

We are dressed in sharp black jackets
and trousers and our ties show the crimp
of confident fingers. It is not strong,
but our cologne mars the air
like a shark's fin. The summer wind
feathers our scalps. We find

a restaurant where Moroccan stew
bends our senses. Potatoes are comets,
yellow onions are long, soft, caresses.
The piano player pulls Satie
from his keys, or Strauss. Everywhere
there is the quiet luster
of buffed marble and brass,
in a muted amber veil. The waiter

brings our drinks, glacial gin,
and the murmured longing
of vermouth. Shock of lemon peel.
I raise the cup without a handle,
and test the wells where I have
swallowed and swallowed
and never drowned.

This is for you, Peter, who found me
when this life had soured
like milk, forgotten or unwanted,
and made me one very cold, dry perfect
martini. That broke my skull open,
that set the earth spinning
like a bright green top.

God's Ears

Michael collects me at five
exactly, asks do I want comfort
food or Mexican. Much as I enjoy
the ubiquitous pleasure of brisket
tucked into enchiladas, tamales
and soft tacos, I wish now

we'd eaten in a place that wasn't
sunken in soothing darkness. We talk
about our writing techniques, early
Scorsese, how Kubrick terrorized
Shelly Duvall on the set
of *The Shining*, how I want
to make a novena for my sister.

Though I'm not Catholic. I will cadge
some mercy from Saint Jude
for Penelope, locked away
and aching, farther from me
than any dying sun.

She swims catastrophe
like a lost fish, and my failures
as a brother keep me company
like disappointed Seraphim.

We get there early for the comedy.
The play is insipid, lines
meticulously remembered still
plummet like poisoned gulls.

Michael leaves at intermission
to grab a couple of beers.
It would take more than this
to rob me of the rush,

the jazz that stokes my breath
on opening night. But I feel Michael's
weariness on the way home. Tangible
as a thick, dull coin in the palm,
knowing it was devotion

that brought him to my door,
when he might have bailed. I hug
Chloe, patting her small belly,
at the same time stroking Kitty-Kitty
who bites my knee, when I rise
to check the mail. Behind the small

door I find another dystopian thriller,
a postcard and coupons. Throughout
the evening I have begged God
to bandage me in the implacable comfort
of His arms, and search my memory

for a past blue lullaby of love
with lyrics like: *spring arrived
on time, but what became of you,*
that will thaw my frail, disaffected
heart. Something sophisticated
and intoxicating and bleak.

Beautiful Boys

I had trouble finding my way
to Michael's party that night.
It was rainy and I was tired,
driving in a part of the city
unfamiliar to me. The streets
were damp. The radio cookin.

Have you ever wondered
about the live DJ on a Saturday
night? The calls that keep him
company? I nursed a bourbon and
water throughout the evening,
genially, told Steven age was just

a number. No one says
how risky it is, to look at the clock.
Sometimes, I think of myself
as a case of arrested development.
Late learning to tie my shoes,
to drive, to stand up for myself,
to drink like a grown up.
Late coming out of the closet.

It was an excellent, soothing
party. Friends who appreciated one
another, hanging, leaning on each other.
Tapping into underground wells
and secret coves.

A skinny poet whose work I enjoyed
was there. His head was shaved,
and though he wore rings in both
ears, I figured he would not be
interested in the way I could touch
his nape or shoulder blades. It was

okay, though, because he was jovial,
and sweet-natured. We were there
to cooperate in each other's gladness
and comfort, trying to get by in a world
that is not always easy to navigate.

I wandered the parking lot, confused
by symmetry. A couple of young men,
asked where the swimming pool was.
They wore shimmering shirts. Blazing
jewelry. I told them I was leaving
a party and lost myself, and couldn't
find my car, or the swimming pool.

They came up close, smiling
sympathetically, explaining
the geography. Looking into my eyes,
exquisite radiance leaking
and spilling, and some kind

of genuine benign boy-lock
going on between us, however
brief. It didn't matter that we
didn't know each other's names,
or the circumstances of that
particular night.

I may be only sixty-four
but I know what love is. We
were just boys. Guys coalescing
in a conspiracy of grins. Beautiful
boys together.

Christopher Stephen Soden received his MFA in Poetry from Vermont College of Fine Arts in January of 2005. He teaches craft, theory, genre and literature. He writes poetry, plays, literary, film and theatre critique for sharpcritic.com and EdgeDallas. Christopher's poetry collection, *Closer* was released by Rebel Satori Press on June 14th, 2011. He received a Full Fellowship to Lambda Literary's Retreat for Emerging LGBT Voices in August 2010. His performance piece: *Queer Anarchy* received The Dallas Voice's Award for Best Stage Performance. *Water and A Christmas Wish* were staged at Bishop Arts and *Every Day is Christmas*

In Heaven at Nouveau 47. Other honors include: Distinguished Poets of Dallas, Poetry Society of America's Poetry in Motion Series, Founding Member, President and President Emeritus of The Dallas Poets Community. His work has appeared in: *Rattle, The Cortland Review, 1111, Typishly, F(r)iction, G & L Review, Chelsea Station, Glitter- wolf, Collective Brightness, A Face to Meet the Faces, Resilience, Ganymede Poets: One, Gay City 2, The Café Review, The Texas Observer, Sentence, Borderlands, Off the Rocks, The James White Review, The New Writer, Velvet Mafia, Poetry Super Highway, Gertrude, Touch of Eros, Gents, Bad Boys and Barbarians, Windy City Times, ArLiJo, Best Texas Writing*

This project was made possible, in part, by generous support from the Osage Arts Community.

Osage Arts Community provides temporary time, space and support for the creation of new artistic works in a retreat format, serving creative people of all kinds — visual artists, composers, poets, fiction and nonfiction writers. Located on a 152-acre farm in an isolated rural mountainside setting in Central Missouri and bordered by ¾ of a mile of the Gasconade River, OAC provides residencies to those working alone, as well as welcoming collaborative teams, offering living space and workspace in a country environment to emerging and mid-career artists. For more information, visit us at www.osageac.org

Osage Arts Community